Ribbons and Roses:

Poetry, Prose, and Potpourri

V. M. WOLTER & JOSEPH A. ZAPALAC

Outskirts Press, Inc.
Denver, Colorado

Ribbons and Roses
Poetry, Prose, and Potpourri
All Rights Reserved.
Copyright © 2009 V. M. Wolter and Joseph A. Zapalac
v4.0

Compiled and Edited Vada M. Wolter
Cover design and photography:Copyright ©2009 Vada M. Wolter - VMW Photography

Scripture quotations are taken from the *Holy Bible, New Living Translation*, copyright ©1996, 2004. Used by permission of Tyndale House Publishers, Inc., Wheaton, Illinois 60189. All rights reserved.

Outskirts Press, Inc.
http://www.outskirtspress.com

ISBN: 978-1-4327-4445-8

Library of Congress Control Number: 2009932028

Outskirts Press and the "OP" logo are trademarks belonging to Outskirts Press, Inc.

PRINTED IN THE UNITED STATES OF AMERICA

Best Wishes!
Prov. 3:5,6
V. Wolter

Contents

Love and Sentimental Section 3 - 47

Joseph and Vada's Introduction

Following our May 22, 1958 graduation from El Campo High School, my former classmate, Vada, and I went our separate ways, never to know the whereabouts of the other, until fate brought us together in the fall of 2008. But that's a story in itself!

Although there are 1,100 miles between us, within five months of being reunited, we caught up on our past lives, became writing partners, and had our first book, *Reflections, Memories Past*, published in March 2009.

The book *Reflections* is a collection of hometown, home-state poetry and prose reflecting the childhood life and memories of Joseph. It represents poetry written with homespun values of love and friendship and was written for the purpose of keeping those memories alive and putting our hometown of El Campo, Texas on the map. Photographs taken by the photographer of the team, Vada, are also included in the book.

Ribbons and Roses: Poetry, Prose, and Potpourri, the book you now hold in your hand, is our second book to be published. The collection within this book contains some childhood memories as well as our thoughts, feelings, and ideas. You will see, too, it goes beyond Texas. You might say "Texas and Beyond."

You may ask how we came up with the title for this book. It's simple! As you look through this book, you will find writings by both Joseph and Vada that carry deep emotion and affection, which tug at the heart much like heartstrings—or *ribbons*. With both of our love for the yellow rose, we had to include *roses*!

You will notice a sprinkling here and there of some *potpourri*, or a delicate bouquet of Scripture from God's Word, the Holy Bible. We believe that everyone needs a bit of "heavenly fragrance" in their lives. You now know the reasoning behind the title of this book.

It is our hope that you will enjoy this collection of various thoughts and ideas of our writings and be inspired as you read each selection. We also hope that you will be stirred to write your own thoughts and feelings.

Blank pages, at the end of each subject category, will give you an opportunity to journal your entries. We feel there is a writer in each person and, with a bit of discipline and encouragement, this can be accomplished. With this being said, all we now have to say is "Write on..."

Faith and Inspirational

"If any of you wants to be my follower, you must turn from your selfish ways, take up your cross, and follow me. If you try to hang on to your life, you will lose it. But if you give up your life for my sake, you will save it. And what do you benefit if you gain the whole world but lose your own soul? Is anything worth more than your soul?"

Matthew 16:24-26

©2008VMWolter   Yellow Rose

The Angel Beside Me

Through the days of
My precious life, short they may be,
There walks beside me an angel,
Whom you cannot see.

She guides me through a straight and narrow path;
I dare not incur her wrath.
I cannot see her, but I know she's there.
In the times of stress, she will care.

I find comfort in dead of night.
I am not alone, even in sleep.
My angel watches closely,
While shadows of night creep.

I wake up, thankful to be alive.
The angel beside me
Has awakened me to see
The light of another day. (JAZ)

Psalm 34: 4-5

"I prayed to the Lord, and he answered me. He freed me from all my fears. Those who look to him for help will be radiant with joy."

Angelica

I dreamed I walked in a peaceful, serene garden.
A beautiful garden surrounded by angels,
Living in heavenly grace,
Surrounded by unbelievable beauty.

There was a beautiful angel picking flowers.
Where have I seen her? I thought,
Looking at her angelic face in awe;
Then I thought of beautiful Angelica.

I lost Angelica many years ago.
She perished in an automobile accident
The day before we were to be married.
I could never forget the memory of her.

The years passed. I took vows of a priest.
In loving memory of her,
I dedicated my life to helping others
And to ease the pain of an empty heart.
I looked at the angel—
Disbelief showing on my face.
Those crystal blue eyes and angelic face
Made her the picture of heavenly bliss.

She glided softly toward me;
Her beautiful smile enchanting me.
This was Angelica—my beloved Angelica.
I knew I was in Heaven.

"Welcome to Heaven, my beloved.
I am your guardian angel.
God has chosen me
To forever be by your side.

You were chosen to visit me
Through your heavenly dream.
Someday, together, we'll walk this path—
After your work on earth is finished."

I could not bring myself to awaken
As I watched my guardian angel,
Resplendent in all her glory,
Stand to bid me farewell.

Deep in thought of my dream,
I walked about my room.
I prepared for church service;
I knew I must hurry.

Suddenly, I felt an invisible presence
Behind me, so real and, yet, I wasn't sure.
I picked up my Bible, turned and
On my desk, saw a small figurine.

It looked familiar, but where had it come from?
I walked toward the figurine and picked it up.
I felt God was telling me that He and Angelica
Would always be by my side. (JAZ)

Country Church

It is a beautiful Sunday morning in a small rural town. The familiar chimes from a small country church bell ring. Some local folks, farmers, and ranchers gather and seat themselves inside the church.

It is early spring. The birds chirp. The grass is lush and green. Inside the church, the priest greets his flock as the service begins. A hush flows over the parishioners as the priest delivers his solemn message from the Bible.

On this particular Sunday morning, I had just arrived in town. It had been many years since my last visit. Once I had lived here. Now I'd come back to relive my youth and to recall once again the many Sunday mornings spent in the small country church.

When church was over, people left slowly. I gathered outside with the others to mix and mingle with these folks. I listened to the chatter as the menfolk and their wives prepared for the day ahead. God, how great it felt to be back with the country folk.

Yes, we were all country folk—like brothers and sisters, through good times, happy, or sad. To this day, I have never forgotten that the Lord is with us forever.

I think back to those nostalgic days. Through trial and error, I learned how to correct my errant ways. I never forgot what I learned in that little church. It was there, in this church, that I learned only too well the principal differences between heaven and hell, but I had to learn the hard way along the road of life.

As the years passed and I found myself growing older, I knew someday my turn must come to leave this mortal life. I have had my chance. I do not despair over my lot in life. Yes, I have lived a life filled with unhappiness and strife. More than once, I stumbled and fell, but I knew that someday I'd pick myself up when God answered the call.

I must confess that I've sinned once in a while, but I never forgot God because I knew he was watching me with his invisible smile. This is why I've come back one more time—to hear that old familiar chime, to recall the memories of my past, and to pay homage to my beloved grandmother (bless her soul), who helped me see the light. (JAZ)

©2008VM Wolter   Pierce Church- Pierce, TX
Pierce Church was built by A. H. "Shanghai" Pierce in the middle 1800s as part of Pierce Townsite. It was relocated in 1981.

Love Letter to Jesus - 01/03/2004

Happy New Year, Lord. I can't believe that I totally forgot to eat black-eyed peas and hominy for breakfast on New Year's Day! What would my little Grandma think? I suppose I'll learn if there is any truth to the fable about eating black-eyed peas and hominy to have money all year.

My thoughts go to my one-and-only sister—how special it is for us that we have each other. I remember growing up in the '40s and '50s and how she was my buddy—my playing partner.

Although, at one point I felt I was too grown up to play with her, so an older cousin and I would run off and hide. Needless to say, Mama found out about this and my cousin and I were punished by having to pull iron weeds. That's something I'll never forget!

We lived in a small wood-framed house that had four rooms and no indoor plumbing or television. We had an outdoor toilet (outhouse) and had to pump our water, but I never felt poor. I was rich with love, family, and good times.

Times were simple and uncomplicated. It was an era when people had time for each other, and a handshake was better than any signed contract.

I am grateful for the time in which I was born and for the treasured memories I have.

I'll close for now. Thank You for the New Year. I pray You will lead and guide our ways and our walk through the year. For what is to come, be with us all and give us strength. Your daughter, (VMW)

A Prayer for Strength

In the early morning of each day
I turn to the precious solitude
That is mine. I take a few moments
To pray over the uncertainties that
Are ahead. And yet, I find solace
From my Bible, which comforts me
In the time of need.
I cannot turn my back on the Good Book.
Strength and courage, I lack,
And everywhere I look,
Adversity is all around.
Yet, deep within my soul
Is salvation that I have found.
This sustains my life's role.

The adversity I face each day,
Brings out the need to sit down and pray.
When you see a smile on my face,
I am happy indeed.
A prayer for strength strengthens,
And faith sees it through. (JAZ)

No Longer the Same

It's dark here! How long must I live in this place?
Nothing but darkness surrounds my face!
Am I not better than this?
I feel the warmth from above.
Is it a feeling of love?
Why can't I see? How long will it be?
Life goes on—I exist. Is there more?
What have I missed?
Wait! Something is happening to me!
I desire to see what is beyond this place.
I feel the sun upon my face.
I've spent a long time in the dark,
But now I'm free...because of Your love for me.
I am no longer the same!
I am a new creature—I have a new name!
Short is my time on earth to sing praises to Thee,
But in my heavenly home, forever I will sing
With other saints, for all eternity. (VMW)

(Inspired while listening to a locust in my backyard)

Sinners live in the dark "underground" until, at an appointed time, they emerge into the light, they cast off the old, and they become new creatures! With joy, they "make noise" to the world around them of their new life and freedom. After a short time, compared to eternity, they are called home, a heavenly home where they continue singing praises to God. (8/5/2003)

Jesus Calls All of Us to Enter His Rest

In Matthew 11:28:30 Jesus tells us to *"Come to Me, all of you who are weary and carry heavy burdens, and I will give you rest. Take my yoke upon you. Let me teach you, because I am humble and gentle at heart, and you will find rest for your souls. For my yoke is easy to bear, and the burden I give you is light."*

How does one enter God's rest? This is best told with an acronym!

Relax
Enter
Submit
Trust

First—slow down and let go of everything—unwind. Just try relaxing with a tight fist. **You can't!** You must let go of what you are holding onto.

Second—we must enter fellowship with God in faith and hope.

Third—submit our will to God, and...

Fourth—trust in God and His promises. (VMW)

Divine Intervention

It seems like yesterday, an unforgettable day,
I was sad that Uncle Sam had sent me far away.
My thoughts were those of an angry young man.
I was angry at Uncle Sam, but off to war I went
to serve my country; Vietnam's where I was sent.

In a land with thick jungles and rice paddies,
I saw faces of the fallen every step of the way.
I faced peril every day.
My faith made me realize God was by my side.

I wanted God to forgive my sins, lessen my fear,
and to help my loved ones who I held so dear.
I wanted to be a good soldier, doing my best.
Time and war would put me through a severe test.

Every passing day, I fought desperately to survive.
I carried a small Bible in my shirt pocket;
It stopped an enemy's bullet and kept me alive.
Intervention kept me going, gave me a will to live.
I believed in God's protection to keep me safe.

Through it all, I survived.
For Divine Intervention, I thanked God and cried.
I returned wearing a badge of honor,
and having to use a crutch.
I didn't mind because of God's kind, gentle touch.
His Divine Intervention brought me home. (JAZ)

Love Letters to Jesus Journal

The following blank pages will provide you with an opportunity to journal your thoughts and feelings as you see God's plan unfold in your life. You might think of this section as your journal in which to write "Love Letters to Jesus" that reflect your deepest thoughts.

Nature and Seasons

"In the beginning God created the heavens and the earth."
Genesis 1:1

Summer

Summer is here! Warm weather, crowded beaches, picnics in the parks, travelers on busy highways—all are a part of summer.

Vacation time at last! It goes by so fast! Your moments under the sun, so swiftly will they pass, but you are having lots of fun.

Basking in leisure on the beach, or fishing quietly on a peaceful lake or just sitting on a bench in the zoo. Ah, yes, this is summer! Golden moments linger everywhere—through our suntans and sunglasses, as we ride our bicycles, or take long walks on lonely trails.

The green leaves of summer. Oh, how we enjoy their shade. We enjoy the sweet taste of ice cream, watermelon, or pop, quenching our thirst.

There are the summer celebrations! Let's not forget July 4th, America's Independence Day and fireworks everywhere! This is summer! (JAZ)

Genesis 8:22

"As long as the earth remains, there will be planting and harvest, cold and heat, summer and winter, day and night."

Ode to 2008

Today marks the end
of 2008, the year—
For, you see,
a new year draws near.

Emotions! There are many.
Emotions! They run high—
Some bring laughter,
While others cause me to cry.

Memories—good and bad—
Written on pages of my heart.
Memories that I never
Want to fade or depart.

The dedication of a baby—
Sweet smelling and soft to hold—
In a quaint little church on a
Sunday morn in January—so cold.

The day in April, she walked down the aisle
My heart bursting with pride;
A day most little girls dream of—
The day they become a blushing bride.

Summer days, hot and humid
And that good ole Texas heat.

The sticky air and mosquitoes
From where there is no retreat.

Then comes September, October
The beginning of fall.
Cool days, cooler nights
And trees swaying in the wind, so tall.

Brisk morning air, I breathe in
While taking my daily tour—
Clear blue skies, cotton ball clouds.
The smell of burning wood—
Memories galore!

Then the day of ECHS Reunion—
1958 the class.
Many attend, some do not
How time passes, so fast.

At the reunion's silent auction, I see
A maroon-colored binder. It calls to me.
It's a book of prose and poetry—
Its author, fellow classmate, Joe Z.

November passes, then comes December
With holiday cheer.
How quickly the year has passed!
The year 2009...so near. (VMW)

Christmas Cheer

Christmas comes but once a year—
a time of beauty and joy.
With it, we celebrate happiness
while children all over eagerly
await the arrival of Santa and his reindeer.
Christmas cheer is everywhere.
'Tis a season to behold,
as the first snow arrives.
Many watch chestnuts roast on an open fire
while basking in the warmth of the living room.

Yes, Christmas is a season of joy.
It's more than the giving of gifts
that mean so much to many
a little girl and boy.
Sometimes we forget
what it's really all about
as we give and receive.

If you stop to think of Christmas past,
of Mary and her boy child,
memories of Christmas will always last.
Our beloved season of joy,
complete with the sound of holiday music
never from our hearts or memory
will we forget Christmas cheer. (JAZ)

September Winds

September winds blow,
charting our course;
for what, we do not know.
My love and I
walk side by side,
holding hands.
There is a tear in her eye
and for me, a heavy heart,
knowing tomorrow we must part.

The scent of autumn is in the air.
The September winds blow,
as we stroll slowly without a care.
The future is ours
and we must fulfill our destiny.
Yet, today, we share our love,
never saying good-bye, just "so long"
under a gentle blue sky,
as the September wind becomes strong. (JAZ)

John 3: 8A

*"The wind blows wherever it wants. Just as you can hear the wind but
can't tell where it comes from or where it is going..."*

A Story Behind the Old Tree

I dreamed about an old tree that once stood proudly in front of my house. I often wondered what it would say if only it could speak. In my dream, this is what it said to me.

Once upon a long-ago time,
        on barren ground I stood,
        a freshly planted tree.
I've lived to be over one hundred years old.
        Listen to what I have to say
        about how I came to be.

I've survived nature's elements
        and witnessed history along the way.
Many were the times when my
        leaves had fallen
        and branches broken.

As I slowly grew through the years,
        I stood in front of a home
        alongside a busy street.
It was a beautiful home filled with love,
        laughing children, friends, and relatives
        who came to meet.

Amidst laughter and joy I stood
        graceful and elegant through
        the spring and summer.

My leaves and branches served as my hood.

Autumn would arrive.
        My leaves would change in the fall.
High above, geese would fly,
heeding nature's call.

Time came to make a change.
        It was a hot summer day
        when branch cutters came,
        and I appeared very strange.

There were overhead power lines.
        My branches had to go.
        My existence would cease
        in a matter of time.

On that fateful day, a heavy rain began to fall.
        With thunder and lightning,
        the darkened sky paid tribute to me—
        a fallen tree.

I awoke from my dream, my emotions running high. Gazing out the living room window, I saw a stump and asked myself, "Why, why, why?" I loved that old tree in my own special way. Dream or no dream, memories of it will linger each day. (JAZ)

Red and Green Tissue Paper

A week before Christmas, Mother started cooking cakes, pies, and, of course, plenty of her cornbread dressing—cooked with the fattest hen.

Daddy and the older boys would butcher the finest hog—our mother usually supervised the sausage making. I can still hear her say, "It needs a little more sage!"

There was lots of ham, bacon, sausage, and lots of relatives and neighbors to share it with. The house was usually full of people from Christmas until after New Year's Day.

The perfect Christmas tree, which Daddy, the older children, and I (the youngest of eight) had walked for hours to find, stood in the old house with its top reaching the tall ceiling. (The time to go choose a Christmas tree is when it's very cold, sleeting, or perhaps snowing a little.)

The decorated tree (a beautiful holly tree with red berries or perhaps a cedar tree) was decorated, for the most part, with red and green paper rope chains draped around the tree. We used a little silver rope for icicles. The last thing to do was to tie big red apples in the tree. We decorated the tree as a family group. Though times were hard—my parents always managed a bushel basket of apples, one of oranges, and one of nuts.

Our stockings were usually hung near the old wood heater. And Santa without fail (nearly always) came through. And always, there in top of our stockings, we found our Christmas present from Santa wrapped in red and green tissue paper.

To this day, seeing red and green tissue paper or holly trees takes me back to those Christmases of long ago.

I remember a few times, our mother worried, "The creeks may rise, and Santa's reindeer won't be able to get across!" When that happened, once or twice, there was always an extra big gift of love and warm family feelings. Mother always saw to that.

From the old family Bible, Coyet and Lillie McKey found encouragement and faith to raise eight children through some very hard times. Today the old family Bible (pages like parchment and badly worn) is put away (wrapped in red and green Christmas paper).

My parents and five of those eight children have gone on. But...I wonder, do they still come for Christmas at the old house with the tall ceilings, a warm fire, and beautiful holly trees with the red berries? Do they hear the laughter of small children and do they remember the red and green tissue paper?

I am thankful for loving parents, a good home life, and these red and green Christmas memories.

—Elsie McKey Overstreet

God is in Control

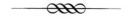

There is no panic in heaven, only plans. That is how God operates. No panic! The Holy Trinity never meets in an emergency session! God has never stepped down from His throne. Jesus has not left His right hand. The Holy Spirit has not stopped interceding for you, His child. Refuse to listen to Satan's lies of fear, discouragement, and despair. You are a victor. God is in control! (VMW)

A Minnesota Lake

I sit alone by a Minnesota lake, deep in thought while writing poetry. It is here where my heart finds peace and serenity—in the state of 10,000 lakes.

It is early spring; there's a chill in the air. The lake is calm, and everything is quiet. In the distance, one can hear the chattering of crows.

I gaze thoughtfully at the trees that stand along the shoreline, awaiting their greenness as Mother Nature and her infinite changes herald the arrival of spring.

The sun is high in the sky, brightening the landscape with its cheery smile, as I write furiously thoughts that come to mind.

Basking in the moments of solitude, on the banks of White Bear Lake, I inhale deeply the clean, fresh air, purging my soul, freeing it from inner turmoil and thanking God for being alive.

The hours pass, not a soul in sight. I sit humble and silent, appreciating the beautiful lake as I continue my vigil by the shoreline, writing to my heart's content.

The silence and serenity of White Bear Lake will soon be broken by passing automobiles. I take one last look at the lake, soon to be filled with boaters and fishermen, before I return home. (JAZ)

A Gentle Rain

It's a gentle rain, falling from an overcast sky. A loud splashing of water is heard as it gushes off the roof to my left, forming a puddle in the flowerbed.

Looking to my right, I see where the rain is coming out an opening where a rain gutter should be, but has been removed. A steady stream flows out, onto the far end of the front lawn's flowerbed. A slight sound can be heard, much like the distant beating of a drum.

A lone teenage girl, dressed in black jeans and a gray tee-shirt, both rain soaked, strolls by; her long, dark hair clings to her face. The question comes to mind, "Why she is walking in the gentle rain?"

The rain has slowed now, except for the smaller stream from the missing gutter. The call of a mourning dove can be heard, in the distance—coo-coo, coo-coo. Other birds can be heard, as well, as if saying, "Thanks, Lord, for the rain. The ground will come to life again."

The call of a dove can be heard over and over again, while another answers, and the distant drums give way now to the calling of the doves—all because of the gentle rain. (VMW)

A California Sunrise

Beautiful indeed is my California sunrise,
as I watch its brilliant glow in early morn.

I ponder my thoughts silently,
gazing wistfully at ocean waves
churning noisily against the shore,
and watching small boats
cruise slowly into harbor.

It's late September.
Gone are the hustle and bustle
of crowds, leaving the
beaches tranquil and deserted,
as a California sunrise appears.

Seagulls fly about.
Their cries pierce the morning air
in their endless search for food.
In the distance,
you hear a tugboat's foghorn,
and see a lighthouse.

I leave the peace and serenity.
My mind is occupied
with memories, past and present,
of summer romance.
I hold no regrets.
With head held high,
I welcome my California sunrise. (JAZ)

Where the Wild Geese Fly

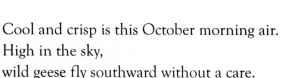

Cool and crisp is this October morning air.
High in the sky,
wild geese fly southward without a care.
They follow their leader.
Their honks are very shrill.
Fall has returned once again
with its welcomed chill.

I stroll about, hands in pockets,
marveling at the change in nature.
Soon my surroundings will be
cloaked with the cover of white,
a crowning touch of winter that draws near.
With a parting look, I view with sadness
as the last of the geese disappear.

Days grow shorter, nights grow longer.
Winter's breath grows stronger.
I look up in the sky.
I wonder—where do the wild geese fly? (JAZ)

Philippians 3:14

*"I press on to reach the end of the race and receive the heavenly prize for
which God, through Christ Jesus, is calling us."*

Solitude on a Distant Shore

I stand alone on a desolate beach, watching a storm gather on the distant horizon. A strong wind blows over the ocean swells. Seagulls fly overhead, their cries echoing above the thunder from the sky, as high waves roll mightily toward the shoreline.

I walk swiftly across the sandy beach, giving an anxious glance toward the darkening sky, feeling the first drops of rain against my face and the heavy force of the wind against my body. "I dare not tarry," I tell myself. "Mother Nature has some work to do, and I'll not stand in her way."

With a crash of thunder and bolts of lightning streaming across the sky, inside a safe haven and out of the rain, I watch Mother Nature vent her fury, thankful to be avoiding her wrath. Her anger will come to pass and I, then, will feel the freedom to walk again on the beach, to enjoy and savor that feeling of solitude. (JAZ)

Welcome to the North Country

Welcome to the North Country, where large trees and lakes abound, amidst tranquility that is seldom found when you live in the big city.

The peaceful woods come alive as rabbits and squirrels scamper through the early morning mist, while deer graze contentedly and the sun rises slowly, chasing away the looming mist.

A loon's cry echoes across a lake and the chirping of birds breaks the stillness of the surroundings as the North Country wilderness awakens.

Welcome to the land of 10,000 lakes—wonderful Minnesota—where the air is fresh and clean and the four seasons greet you with nature's best. (JAZ)

Sitting Alone

Sitting alone on a park bench, amidst the peaceful surroundings of a park in White Bear Lake, I watch gentle waves roll slowly toward the shoreline; splashing against the small rocks on the shore's edge.

'Tis an early fall morning—it is very quiet, except for the babble of crows, echoing across White Bear Lake, which is free from boaters and fishermen. You feel the autumn chill, and a slight breeze awakens you from your deep thoughts as you prepare for the day.

You watch little ducks swimming in the lake, and an occasional bird fly idly toward an unknown resting place. You gaze toward the woods, which surround the park, soon to change color with the advent of fall, and you realize that the autumn of your life is about to pass.

What more could you ask from nature while sitting alone, free from troubles and the weight of society's problems? Mother Nature beckons you to behold the beauty that is meant to be. I must now leave and continue my journey in search of new challenges that are ahead. (JAZ)

The Burning Bush

By the side of my home stands a solitary burning bush. I love it so well. How long will it continue to mature? This I cannot tell! From spring-green to autumn-red; my burning bush will change with every day that comes to pass. I pause for a moment to admire you, my burning bush. Oh, how I bask in your beauty, natural and true. You stand wondrous in all your glory as you continue to grow very tall! Yes, burning bush, you are so immaculate amongst the golden leaves of fall!

I do not welcome your transformation as Mother Nature makes her annual change. One by one your leaves will fall and you'll appear barren and strange. Your growth will continue, this I do not fear. Winter will arrive with a relentless push. Fear not, my beautiful burning bush. The landscape will be covered with snow, but you will survive to grow and once again, regain your natural beauty. (JAZ)

Fall

Fall has arrived.
It is a colorful time of year
When trees shed their leaves.
The days become shorter,
And evening's chill sets in.
Couples walk briskly,
Reflecting silently,
Breathing nature's fresh air.

Autumn, sweet autumn!
A nostalgic time of year that
Brings out the best in us,
Making us realize another year has passed.

Beautiful fall!
As the cool air settles,
One's pace is quickened.
The moon peers downward,
Through the multitude of clouds.
Welcome back, fall. (JAZ)

The Woodsman

Living alone in the forest thick, the woodsman stays in the midst of the creatures, large and small. His world is the contentment of a bonding with nature.

His small cabin is surrounded by towering trees, and free from the encroachment of society, civilization, and man. He rules his domain in the woods, not as a hunter but as a free soul.

He is at peace with himself amongst the creatures, great and small; he walks and is a witness to the four seasons, watching each change. For many years, he's lived in the woods and has yet to see a hunter. Deep in his heart, he knows he must leave one day, leaving behind forever his world.

The woodsman has grown older. Daily he ambles through the woods, his step no longer brisk. The health he once enjoyed, among his peaceful surroundings, diminishes slowly.

In the light of an early morning, the woodsman walks a short distance to a peaceful lake amongst towering pine trees and stops to rest against the trunk of a large tree.

As he rests, he listens to the loon's call echoing across the lake. He watches deer scamper about, and he knows his time has come. The woodsman closes his eyes for the final time, a peaceful smile on his rugged face. (JAZ)

The Shores of Lake Michigan

Winds of change blow softly
along the shore of Lake Michigan.
Fall is in the air.
The year is drawing slowly to a close.
I stand alone on a deserted beach,
deep in contemplation.
While listening to waves splashing
against the shoreline
and watching seagulls hover above,
I wonder what the future holds.

Change is inevitable.
As the seasons change, so must I.
In my peaceful solitude,
my thoughts dwell on past and present
of what could have been but never will be
and deep within me lies this question
Would I do it again?
The answer does not come easily.
To that question, I shall not be blind
as I continue my stroll along the shore of Lake
Michigan. (JAZ)

The Vanishing Year

How quickly the four seasons pass.
How swiftly the year ends.
It seems like it just arrived.
You remember spring's fresh touch
and enjoy the beauty of nature.
Summer, wonderful summer—
the good old summertime
and the joys of the outdoors.
Before long, September winds blow
and the golden touch of autumn
will cover our landscape with fallen leaves,
a reminder that winter is close behind.
In a matter of time, everyone will say good-bye
to the vanishing year. (JAZ)

Winter in the North Woods

As the strong winds from the north blow, after the last leaves of autumn have fallen, Mother Nature lets everyone know that the icy touch of winter will soon be upon us.

The ground is now covered with snow. From inside our cabin, we bask in the warmth from the fireplace, and gaze through the window at the serenity of winter in the north woods.

The day passes and evening is upon us. The cold, clear night is illuminated by a full moon and its light peers downward through the trees, casting faint shadows onto the snow-covered ground. Nothing breaks the stillness of the beautiful wilderness evening. This is winter in the north woods. (JAZ)

December

'Tis that time of year.
Everyone is of good cheer
and snow has fallen,
gracing our landscape
with nature's white.

It won't be long now,
before Santa comes around
on his annual trek
and happiness and joy abound,
on Christmas Day.

Blazing fireplaces, roasting chestnuts
and a decorated tree, surrounded by gifts,
make for a happy family.
December, indeed,
is a month to remember.

As each Christmas goes by, we grow older.
We gaze out the window,
admiring December's beauty.
Forever in our hearts
will remain the memory
of a very special season. (JAZ)

©2008VM Wolter – Divine Radiance – Stafford, TX

Love Letters to Jesus Journal

The following blank pages will provide you with an opportunity to journal your thoughts and feelings as you see God's plan unfold in your life. You might think of this section as your journal in which to write "Love Letters to Jesus" that reflect your deepest thoughts pertaining to nature and the beauty seen in God's creation.

Love and Sentimental

"Love is patient and kind. Love is not jealous or boastful or proud or rude. It does not demand its own way. It is not irritable, and it keeps no record of being wronged. It does not rejoice about injustice but rejoices whenever the truth wins out. Love never gives up, never loses faith, is always hopeful, and endures through every circumstance."
1 Corinthians 13:4-7

Before Leaving

There's no need to say a last good-bye. Deep in our young hearts, fond memories of each other will remain. We both knew you wanted to leave. Your future is bright, your star shines on the horizon, and I'll love you, nevertheless. What I really wanted you to know is that a good-bye doesn't mean the end of love. However, your absence means I'll miss that smiling face that is you.

Before you leave, we'll draw close to each other in a lover's embrace. We'll clasp hands tightly, bonded in love and cherished friendship. We'll both struggle to hold back our tears, which are certain to come. Tears of love that flow from our eyes will never wash away the love in our hearts as the winds of change beckon for you to go. I, too, must anticipate the call of my destiny, which awaits me on the distant horizon.

Before leaving, there are sad smiles, hushed tones. Once more, we cling to each other, our kisses gentle and firm. Our love is true. Our faith is unshaken as we stand before the ocean. A gentle breeze blows ocean spray in our faces, two lovers saying good-bye—before leaving. (JAZ)

Chivalry

In the dungeon of a troubled mind, I await the arrival of a tomorrow that is unknown to me. I lie awake in fear that permeates my soul, or is it uncertainty that haunts—perhaps a threat of doom that weakens my faith and strength in my body.

I curse the demons that strive for possession and, yet, morrow's early light will shine. I must gather my strength to carry on the goodness within me. It is then, and only then, I must face the inevitable.

I do not travel alone on my perilous journey, oh so far away, for God's at my side, unseen, unheard, but I can sense his invisible touch. He will guide me across troubled waters, despite the foes that sorely stand in my way, to seek, and ask for, the hand of a fair young maiden.

I have fought many battles and led many charges, proving that I am worthy of her love—or am I? I ask myself, "Am I a knight of honor and respect? Shall I be as a stone unturned?" Her love is what I seek, but a battle must be fought for her honor, and my bravery proven once again.

Yes, I am a knight of love, and I must once again accept the challenge of saber and sword, putting on my coat of honor, making ready my beloved steed, and preparing for the battle that's before me. Death awaits the man who falls.

The day of retribution has come. I now defend my fair maiden. Her honor and hand await me. Should I fall, my battle will be over. If not, I shall reign as a man with a Christian heart and my betrothed, yielding my weapon of death.

On the field of battle, underneath a cloudy gray sky, two knights meet. Unquestioned is their bravery. Chivalry and courage reign and soon the air rings with the clash of steel—blade against blade. The clash of titans fighting for the heart of a woman, and then comes silence.

The challenge of honor has been satisfied. A brave warrior spills slowly, but he will live. No longer shall I wave my sword in battle, for the time has come to claim my fair maiden's hand and never again take another man's life. (JAZ)

Face to Face With One Another

You are like a mystery to me, my sweet San Diego woman. You and I, young and fancy free on a California shoreline. We had briefly met. There we were, face to face with one another, and if only time could have stopped for a while before your beautiful face became a blur.

We were strangers, you and I, until the moment came when we looked at each other, eye to eye, unabashed and without playing a game. San Diego woman, with golden hair and a face so fine, you've captured my heart. If only our time together could have lasted forever. Alas, it wasn't meant to be for us—two strangers, young and vibrant. (JAZ)

If I Tried

If I tried, no matter what I'd say
I could not have had a better day.
From beginning to the very end,
You were the best, my dear friend.

If I tried explaining, who'd understand?
We play all the music...no need for a band!
Music of yesteryear, rock and roll,
Coming deep from within the soul.

If I tried turning over a new page
From the book, now brittle with age,
What mysteries would I find?
Only a chord that does bind.

A chord, though invisible, that's very strong;
It holds us each day, and all night long.
It's held us together on the days I cried.
A better friend, I couldn't find—if I tried. (VMW)

Closer Than a Brother

"There are 'friends' who destroy each other, but a real friend sticks closer than a brother." Proverbs 18:24

Because of You

I remember the beauty I saw in your eyes.
Your memory, I shall not forget.
My heart does not tell lies.
Once in a while my heart aches with pain.
Because of you—from my eyes, tears fall like rain.

Because of you—I hope and pray
through each long day and night
that I will once again see you some day.
Although I wait patiently with an empty heart,
I know that a tomorrow for both of us
will come and bring us a new start.

Because of you—my love
for both of us will never dissipate.
Sometimes an absence makes the heart
grow fonder. After your return,
all is forgiven—said and done—
then our separation may have been for better,
and it was all because of you. (JAZ)

Lovers Apart

On a hot summer day,
I lie on a beautiful California beach,
thinking of you, oh so far away—
if only you were within reach.
You're not! I know what to do
while I lie basking underneath the hot sun,
thinking of you.

Our past filled with fun, of times shared
between two lovers who really cared.
Two lovers now apart,
several thousand miles away
from each other's heart.
Perhaps it's best for one another
to once in awhile get away to think things over,
renewing our sense of direction.
I have no doubt in mind what I intend to do
after leaving my beautiful California.
I will come back and marry you. (JAZ)

Letter to Melody Blue

Dear Melody,
You and I will never forget 1958—
an unforgettable year for me.
I remember our first date,
our fun times, and our first kiss,
our treasured past, moments of bliss—
precious memories that last—
our teenage years and small arguments,
this filled your eyes with tears.

There came a time
you and I broke up; you began to cry
as the moment came for us to say "Good-bye."
I write this letter to you,
my dear beloved Melody Blue,
something in my heart told me
this is what I must do.
In writing this letter, Melody Blue,
my heart feels better because I still love you. (JAZ)

True Love

Your eyes sparkle, like the diamonds in your ring.
Your demure smile, and come-hither look,
And alluring lips show who you really are.

Because of our love for each other,
Only the look in our eyes—words unspoken—
Reveals the meaning of true love shared.
It's a treasure deep within us that withstands
The swift passage of time—this is true love. (JAZ)

Six Questions

"I feel the need to write, to put my thoughts and feelings down in black and white—not just *feel* what I'm feeling, but to be able to *see* the words, as they flow from my heart!"

In the early morning hours, my eyes caught a glimpse of a word here and there being written. Was I reading correctly, or reading something into the message? I don't know; perhaps I'll never know. But the emptiness and loneliness that followed were real, as were the many tears.

At first, they came silently. Like tiny, salty streams, they ran down my cheeks, falling onto my breast. I wanted to stop them, but even more I wanted to open the floodgates and let emotions run rampant.

Finally, the floodgates opened and the salty streams flowed more freely. My heart felt as if it had been shattered into a million pieces!

I ask myself, why? Why am I feeling this way? I don't know, nor can I explain.
What has caused this unbearable ache? Is it a feeling of change that has come about?

Who's responsible? Is it me? You? Perhaps both?

When did it all begin? More unanswered questions!

Where will this bad feeling lead if not controlled? The answer comes—Heartbreak Hotel.

How will I be able to accept change and go forward? The answer—it won't be easy! Yet, I must as hopes and dreams unfold and the sweetness of success is tasted. Oh, the price one pays for success! I wonder, is it worth it? (VMW)

When I Am Resentful

"A stone is heavy and sand is weighty, but the resentment caused by a fool is even heavier." Proverbs 27:3

My Dear Eloise

There is nothing stronger than a bond between people who love each other. Our friendship has been tested through good times and sad, just like sister and brother, or a husband and wife. We stood side by side in life's dark corridors.

We've grown older, you and I. We live on opposite sides of this wonderful country. No matter the distance, what lives in our hearts is the friendship between us. You lost your husband. I lost my wife. Years would pass before hurt would leave, but fate dealt us a kind hand for the morrow that approaches. We'll meet again, my dear Eloise. (JAZ)

Memory

He strolled along the beach,
a young man deep in thought;
the ocean's water within reach.
There were answers he desperately sought
to questions that lay deep within.
He gazed at the distant horizon
with a far-off look in his eyes.

The late afternoon sun began to sink.
Above, the cries of seagulls. He walked alone,
giving him time to think
of the good times he once had on this beach.
Now those good times were over,
never again to be within his reach.

He knew he could not bring back the past.
From him, his only love gone—
leaving a memory that would last.
As he gazed at the darkened sky above,
his solitude and desolation
granted him a small measure of peace
to think of what had been
and now was only a memory. (JAZ)

*"The Lord is my strength and my shield. I trust him with all my heart.
He helps me, and my heart is filled with joy. I burst out in songs of
thanksgiving." Psalm 28:7*

The Reconciliation

It is a Friday, the end of the workweek.
Driving home, tired, weary, and empty,
you pull into your driveway and get out.
Walking toward the mailbox,
you reach inside and pull out a letter
from your estranged wife—
a lady down on love.
You know what she wants
from the countless letters written.

You mutter something under your breath
as you walk inside your empty living room.
No one is there to greet you—
no one to talk to, except yourself,
about the many lonely days behind you.
You walk to the kitchen.
Opening the refrigerator, you pull out a drink
and sit down in a comfortable chair
to enjoy a few moments of solitude.

A few minutes will pass
before you open and read the letter,
while you drink from your glass
and ponder what has been written
by your ex. You finish your first drink,
contemplating another,
while letting your thoughts sink

in about that letter you received
and that question from her.
"How about a reconciliation?"
Your heart skips a beat
as your mind sinks into deep thought
of a love and marriage, oh so sweet,
and the good time—and bad—
and the split between you and her.
Maybe it was for the best
to be separate and let love heal
deep wounds, and then let time do the rest.
Yet, that letter and that magic word
"reconciliation" make you happy.

You have her number! Give her a call!
You place your drink aside
in anticipation of hearing her voice.
She answers in a pleasant, sweet voice,
without bitterness and anger.
Both of you talk, just like old friends,
like a husband and wife,
and lovers you had once been.
The longer you talk,
reconciliation is certain.

Saturday came early.
Your heart carried a jubilant beat
as you packed your car
to travel downstate to see your former sweet,
knowing everything would be alright.
You two would rekindle love in the dead of night,
wiping away old hurts and enjoying reconciliation.
(JAZ)

A Lady Named Elizabeth Street

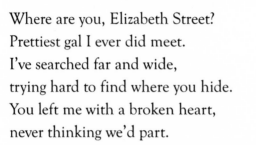

Where are you, Elizabeth Street?
Prettiest gal I ever did meet.
I've searched far and wide,
trying hard to find where you hide.
You left me with a broken heart,
never thinking we'd part.
Long are my days, you had your ways,
but I keep searching, Elizabeth Street,
until we once again meet.

You left me for another,
a man I called my brother.
I don't know what to do.
I do not hate him, but I still love you.
Comes the morrow,
I'll still pace the floor in sorrow,
for I truly loved you—
a love I truly knew.
But, you left me, Elizabeth Street.
My heart aches. For you,
it will forever beat,
my dear and beloved Elizabeth Street. (JAZ)

Treasured Memories

I purge, from my once unhappy soul,
the memories of what had been
and never will be again.
Yet, treasured memories past,
deep in my heart, forever will last.

Treasured memories that erase
the bitterness and unhappiness,
harbored inside me for many years.
I consider myself lucky to have stood
in the rain that washed away tears
in my life that once seemed bleak.

I look forward to the future.
I'm buoyant in spirit,
my heart and mind unclouded;
the will to live, strong—
never again to bend to weakness.
I pursue destiny, unmindful
of what fate has in store for me. (JAZ)

"We can make our plans, but the Lord determines our steps." *Proverbs 16:9*

Whatever Happened to the Good Old Days?

Time shows no respect!
When you wonder about
those good old days,
no matter where you live,
no city or town too small,
but the fact remains—
you've grown older.

Years ago, life was slower.
Now, it's fast paced.
Everything about it
is something you have not faced,
but life isn't the same
when change does come.
Isn't that a shame?

Gone are the days of dime popcorn
and quarter movies;
even the 29-cent a gallon gasoline.
The innocence of past time is lost!

Yes, the '20s through the '60s
are gone forever, but they live
in mind, memory, song, and longevity.
What we cannot change, we accept.
Growing older is a way of life.
Sad, but true, we'll always wonder...

whatever happened to the good old days? (JAZ)

©2008 VM Wolter – Peace Lily, Stafford, TX

When I Don't Want to Repeat My Mistakes

"Don't copy the behavior and customs of this world, but let God transform you into a new person by changing the way you think. Then you will learn to know God's will for you, which is good and pleasing and perfect." Rom 12:2

"Take delight in the Lord, and he will give you your heart's desires. Commit everything you do to the Lord. Trust him, and he will help you. He will make your innocence radiate like the dawn, and the justice of your cause will shine like the noonday sun." Psalm 37:4-6

Table for Two

Such a lovely couple they make! They come, daily, to the same table at the same time. Just look at them! You can tell they love one another!

One day the lady doesn't show. A second and third day goes by... still she doesn't show. Soon it's been a week, a month!

Yet, the man faithfully continues to come daily, and sit at the same table at the same time, patiently waiting.

This is how Jesus is! He is there waiting for your arrival and to spend time with you. He is patient, kind, forgiving, and he loves you! (VMW)

Love Letters to Jesus Journal

The following blank pages will provide you with an opportunity to journal your thoughts and feelings as you see God's plan unfold in your life. You might think of this section as your journal in which to write "Love Letters to Jesus" that reflect your deepest thoughts pertaining to love, feelings, and emotions.

Philosophy

"Don't let anyone capture you with empty philosophies and high-sounding nonsense that come from human thinking and from the spiritual powers of this world, rather than from Christ." Colossians 2:8

Philosophy

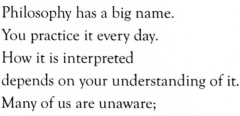

Philosophy has a big name.
You practice it every day.
How it is interpreted
depends on your understanding of it.
Many of us are unaware;
sometimes others don't care—
not realizing what philosophy is.

Philosophy is the way we live it.
It is our guideline in life every day.
How philosophy is applied
depends on you and your goals.
Your beliefs stem from early childhood.
In growing older, you become wiser.
There are certain rules in life
and philosophy applies to them.

Your life is your philosophy—
the things you've come to know and learn.
One man's philosophy is another's ignorance
if not properly understood.
Intelligence comes through philosophy learned
through meaningful experience.
It's a precious gift received.
This is philosophy, lived and learned. (JAZ)

One Man's Philosophy

I cannot reap what I have not sown.
In life, we have goals, hopes, and dreams;
we think about them daily.
Some of us fail in our desire to achieve,
others succeed.
Behind success comes the taste of sweet wine—
or sour grapes.
Of what I have accomplished, I can be proud.
Yet, through failure I've learned in life,
nothing is handed to you on a silver platter.
I'll stumble and fall only to pick myself up again.
This is the difference between success and failure.
(JAZ)

Life's Crossroads

Life's crossroads are many. They are filled with twists and turns. Lost are the few who are uncertain of which direction to go. Wiser they will be once they know they've found the right way. Life's crossroads will not be difficult to cross once there's a sense of direction. It's a common fact that everyone makes a wrong turn; no matter what or where that crossroad might be. It behooves us to stop, look, and listen before we venture into unknown paths. It's then, and only then, you'll have learned well the lessons of life and life's crossroads. (JAZ)

Stories in Our Lives

With each passing day in our life,
There remains behind a story to be told.
If we could remember everything
That we hold dear to us,
It would be interesting to see our
Stories appear in a book.

We live life in many different ways.
The stories in our lives,
If read from a book,
Would seem unbelievable.
Yet, each chapter comes to life
As the reader turns each page.

Everything we do in life
Has a beginning, middle, and end.
We live and experience life as it unfolds.
It doesn't matter who we are,
What we do, or where we go—
There'll always be stories in our lives. (JAZ)

"Trust in the Lord and do good. Then you will live safely in the land and prosper. Commit everything you do to the Lord. Trust him, and he will help you." Psalm 37:3, 5

The Best is Yet to Come

The best is yet to come—
maybe next week, perhaps later.
The years will pass
before the best years of your life
show what existence has accomplished.

We strive in this life
to accomplish meaning to it.
Every day is a daily pattern.
The habits in our daily lives change
continually with different perspectives.

Sometimes we wait longer than others.
Sometimes we feel our efforts are in vain,
and yes, we do become impatient
as we try to realize our goals
that result either in success or failure.

Wishful thinking, unfulfilled dreams,
disappointments galore!
It seems life has treated you unkindly.
Do not despair for the best is yet to come. (JAZ)

Life

In everyday life, it takes sadness
to make our happiness reappear,
causing one's gladness to
chase away the perpetual tear.

Just like a rainbow in the sky
after a gentle rain,
no more will you cry
and suffer pain.

Through life and death, we have a role.
It is never too late to examine your soul—
to see what you are missing in life—
that, in today's world, is filled with strife.

It is a different world today
and everyone must hope and pray
that life for us will, for a season,
hold rhyme and reason.

Life is a journey everyone travels.
Sometimes, without rhyme and reason, it unravels.
Keep in mind, we mustn't fall apart;
we must have faith and a strong heart.
No matter what, it's still a wonderful life. (JAZ)

Life's Rocky Road

Throughout my existence,
I've walked life's lonesome road.
I walked alone; no one could walk it for me.
Upon my shoulders, I carried a load.
A vision of my life, I couldn't foretell or see.

I would stray along the way,
Missing paths, more than one turn or two.
Life's rocky road proved a challenge each day.
Yes, I'd stumble and fall,
but I knew if I were a real man
I'd stand up and face life's call
and that heaven would be my home. (JAZ)

Happy Is the Man

"Those who listen to instruction will prosper; those who trust the Lord will be joyful." Proverbs 16:20

Changing Times

The cost of living is out of sight!
Life's problems fill me with fear.
I gave up my carefree way of life,
because I have finally seen the light.
But all is not doom and gloom.
The future does not seem very bright;
this includes trying to escape earth's problems
with pollution and blight.
Still, it behooves us to remain positive
and keep our goals in sight.

Sometimes I feel like an iron-clad knight—
bold, brave, and facing today's challenges.
I fight the noble fight.
Changing times, this is what they are.

It is difficult to keep from being uptight.
Sometimes I wish I were a kite,
soaring high in the sky far from sight.
By dark of night or light of day,
I'd ascend with great delight.

You cannot escape the problems
of the world and get very far.
Still I wish I were a kite.
I'd escape these changing times
by being held by string, clutched
by a firm hand, letting me fly gracefully
under a sun, o so bright! (JAZ)

Confidence

I can't gaze into a crystal ball
and predict what the future will hold.
I must follow my call.
I must be brave and bold,
letting destiny guide me
through uncertainty that awaits me.
Following the light, I must see
in darkness late.
I must not be blind
to the direction I follow.
I tell my mind
my dreams aren't hollow,
in a voice strong and loud.
Confidence, sweet confidence,
that makes me stand tall and proud.
Confidence on my shoulders I carry
far along the road of life
I shall not tarry in this world,
filled with daily strife.
I've learned my lessons well.
Yes, only time will tell
if my confidence will succeed—or fail. (JAZ)

Chaos and Confusion

In the midst of chaos and confusion,
I stand alone, seeking rhyme and reason.
Questions are many, answers few.
But wise is the man who seeks solution
and wisdom that defy confusion.
The bold thinker must remain unafraid;
the weak thinker must gather strength
through patience, perseverance
and courage to face reality.

For it is I and others like me
who struggle daily against adversity,
against many odds.
Yes, my friends, heed my mortal words
that someday will ring true.
Words of wisdom that chase away chaos and
confusion, sending those dark forces
from whence they came.
Welcome into your life wisdom,
the mother of survival, in troubled times.
I now know of what I speak.
I, the philosopher and the master
of his own philosophy,
triumph over chaos and confusion.
I am strong because of my God-given gift! (JAZ)

Love Letters to Jesus Journal

The following blank pages will provide you with an opportunity to journal your thoughts and feelings as you see God's plan unfold in your life. You might think of this section as your journal in which to write "Love Letters to Jesus" that reflect your deepest thoughts pertaining to your philosophy (attitude, viewpoint, idea, values) on life.

Potpourri

"But thank God! He has made us his captives and continues to lead us along in Christ's triumphal procession. Now he uses us to spread the knowledge of Christ everywhere, like a sweet perfume. Our lives are a Christ-like fragrance rising up to God."
II Corinthians 2: 14-15a

The Search

Through mountains, valleys,
wilderness and barren land,
the lone horseman rode his trusty steed,
sometimes through snow or rain.
To these, he was no stranger without rest.
By day or night, the search continued,
undaunted, unafraid in his quest.
A man obsessed. He faced many a danger
through the wild and wooly west.
He knew his day would come,
placing his gunman's skill to the test.
The rider realized he couldn't return home.
His destiny he could not spurn.
Doing what must be done;
his search would finally end with peace of mind.
(JAZ)

A Farmer's Lament

Day after day, from early morning to night,
I work a schedule that is very tight.
I am a land farmer who spends time in the field.
I plant crops in soil that may or may not yield.
Sometimes I think what I do is in vain.
Oftentimes, I sit long and hard on my tractor,
praying for rain.

Then, I come home at the end of the day.
At the supper table, the family begins to pray.

Each night, when dishes have been put away,
my family sits on the front porch, with much to say.
I sit in my chair, my old dog by my side,
viewing my family with pride.
I gaze at the stars in the skies,
all around are many mosquitoes and fireflies.
Tomorrow comes early. It's getting late,
and I must attend to the crops that wait.

It seems prayers were answered the very next day.
I've found that it pays to pray.
The rains came, the rains went.
Certainly they were a blessing, heaven sent.

I've farmed this land for many years,
through good times and bad, and shed many tears.

A farmer's lament is easy to understand,
especially when trying to farm his land.
Yet, all in all, through hard work,
I found my way of life rewarding and very grand.
If I had to do it all over,
I would—if I were a younger man! (JAZ)

No Regrets

I've traveled on many rocky roads,
strayed from narrow paths,
charting my course through life—
without any regrets.

My trials were many.
Nothing came easy.
Through difficult times,
I struggled for survival,
and to this day—
I have no regrets.

It wasn't easy growing up.
I've discovered life's pleasures,
and its disappointments.
I've enjoyed success,
measured in small losses.
Needless to say—
I have no regrets. (JAZ)

Same Story, Different People

Wherever I travel, no matter who I meet, I listen to people who have something to say—even to neighbors living across the street. This makes for an interesting day.

Everyone has a story they want to tell. Some stories are difficult to believe, but you listen anyway, because that story may become a book that you may someday sell.

More than once, I've listened to stories told of and about people, sad and true. Deep inside, my feelings turned cold. Sometimes I wouldn't know what to say or do.

It's not difficult for me to listen to people talk about personal woes, and troubled lives. But to help them, I cannot, as they tell me about life's highs and lows.

I cannot ask questions from people I haven't met.   Strangers understand what I have to say and listen as well, their mind set on telling the same story.

Yes, stories repeat themselves through coincidence. They are told by everyday people, near and far. Some are happy, others are sad, about people who have fallen along the way beneath the glitter of a faraway story. (JAZ)

The Poem

Every poem tells a story.
Whether short, long, bitter, or sweet,
It's written from feelings within—
emotions, which carry us
through a wondrous world.
It takes a creative imagination
to paint a picture with words,
magical words, which flow smoothly,
staying on course with rhyme and rhythm.

A poem is more than just a poem;
it's a song from the heart.
From the song comes a story.
As the story grows longer,
it becomes a book.
From that book come many chapters, read by many.
It doesn't matter where you live,
your mind is enriched by knowledge;
this becomes wisdom.
You are rich indeed, all because of a poem. (JAZ)

The Old Home

An old home stands silent and empty.
Surrounding it is barren land
that once yielded many a bountiful crop.
The old home stands alone;
its mournful appearance overlooks
an open road, soon to be widened.

I wonder about that old home,
for I know what will become of it.
I stand silent, feeling alone deep
inside because I once lived in it.
I've now returned once more
to a past that housed my youth.

While gazing at that home—
an aging frame structure
subjected to ravages
of time and nature's elements—
I recall a special time.
While standing in eerie silence,
I think of wonderful days within that home.

I walk inside this empty house,
a lump wells in my throat.
The windows are broken and dust covers
the creaky floors in every room
where my family and I once lived.

I stroll through each room,
erasing from memory what had once been.
I take a lasting look at the old house.
Trying hard not to look back,
on this cold, windy day,
I bid farewell to my past! (JAZ)

The Yellow Rose

When I think about my Yellow Rose

Of Texas, my heart cries.

Each time I think about her,

The memory of her never dies.

When spring comes,

The wildflowers of Texas come alive;

April showers bring out the beauty of the landscape.

My thoughts of her are not in vain.

I'll see her again someday,

And I'll not feel any pain (JAZ)

The Grocery Store

I sit alone in silence on a small bench
inside a busy grocery store.
In and out pass busy shoppers
through the store's front door.
From different walks of life
these people come,
with cash for purchases and
credit cards for some.
Without being obvious,
I study their faces—
these unknown strangers
from different places.

They pay no attention to me.
I am just a solitary observer, you see.
I watch pretty ladies,
some not so pretty, come and go,
looking like they're ready to go to a picture show.
As for me, an aged fellow named Joe,
I could not think of a better way to idle
time and escape from the extremely humid heat.
This is why I occupy a grocery store seat.

I hate to walk down the supermarket's aisle.
Every step I take feels like a mile.
I have to choose my path carefully
to keep from being run over by a speeding

shopper and their grocery cart.
Not too great for me with my aging heart.
Finally, I get up to buy groceries,
not forgetting an extra loaf of bread.
From this grocery store
I will leave, my wallet empty.
This is my day at the grocery store—
nothing more is to be said. (JAZ)

The Invisible Knight

Sleep well, my beloved princess.
I am your guardian, day and night.
My love grows stronger for you every day.
You cannot see me with mortal sight.
I am the invisible knight, bold and brave.
I guard you, my beloved princess,
From enemies that would enslave.
I, your invisible knight,
Am prepared for battle.
For your love and honor, my sword
Against the enemy shall rattle.
You cannot see me. Yet in your dreams,
I am yours forevermore.
Someday we'll become one in heaven's open door.
Sleep well, dearest princess.
For, I, the invisible warrior,
Shall always love you. (JAZ)

The Stories That Kids Tell

I remember those days of yesteryear,
when I was just a kid who told stories.
Some were true, some were made up.
The stories I told were enough
to try one's imagination,
especially the stories I heard from others.

There was the time I beat
the best marble shooter around.
After the shooting stopped,
there were no marbles on the ground.

My, how my pockets would bulge
while my friend's pockets were empty.
The joys of being a champion marble shooter!
But wait, there is more to tell.

There was a story I would tell
about the "Boogie Man."
But I ended up scaring myself
and others as well,
especially when Halloween came around.

My grandmother told me stories
about a troll that lived under a bridge.
To this day, I respect all bridges!
I've grown older, and yet,
I cannot forget some of the stories
that kids love to tell. (JAZ)

©2009 VM Wolter – Wharton County Bridge, TX
On a memory-lane-revisited trip, I took this photo as Joseph drove over this
bridge on our way to our hometown. We both shook in our boots, recalling the
stories we'd heard about it.

©2009 VM Wolter –Troll Bridge, Wharton County, TX
Joseph and I, both, have always had respect for bridges, and the eerie feeling we
get from just looking at this photograph speaks volumes to us.

The Cold, Gray Wall

I stood in front of that cold, gray wall, filled with names of warriors who answered their country's call. I couldn't help but shed a tear for those men who fought in Vietnam—who no longer know the meaning of fear. Their names are on the cold, gray wall staring back at me.

I shiver deep inside, thinking of that war, which was meant to keep a country communist free. Regardless of which side was right or wrong, both sides fighting through day and night paid a horrific price.

The wall does not smile; its cold reflection of my face shows tears. As I trace the names, I take medals from my pocket and place them gently on this hallowed ground.

I weep openly at the wall, with hope that never again brave men will fall for a cause in vain. As the rain falls gently, I turn to leave, not looking back, my heart saddened. I know where I must go, for there is a new life ahead, and never again will I fight. I say farewell to the wall as I struggle with my emotions to face the journey ahead. (JAZ)

Country Memories

I walked through many fields in youthful days.
My dog and I crossed many pastures.
Through wooded groves and cotton fields,
we'd roam under a hot Texas sun.
We'd bask in the peaceful countryside
while hunting for small game.

I enjoyed watching the flight of a lone eagle
soaring above in a clear blue sky,
his sharp eyes scanning the ground for prey.
What a pleasure it was to listen to the crows
chatter nosily in the distance, and to hear
the clear, whistling song of a meadowlark.

How I long to relive those golden days—
a time when life was simple on the farm
and youthful innocence grew with nature,
in fields, pastures, and woods of home.
I recall the muddy creeks and blueberry patches
where my dog and I once roamed.

It's nice to enjoy memories of the past,
of a time that never seemed to last.
Some things in your heart will change,
but, deep inside is that youth that
never forgets those country memories. (JAZ)

©2009VM Wolter JMorton Barn, FM 1300 TX
Gone are the days I spent climbing the hay bales Daddy stored in this barn and watching him milk the cows. Soon it will be no more, but the memories linger on forever in my heart.

©2009VM Wolter Zapalac Barn, El Campo, TX
Almost gone, but certainly not forgotten. On our recent visit to El Campo, Texas and to this barn of Joseph's childhood, a swarm of killer bees met us, and we made a quick departure—just some of the hazards of being writers and a photographer.

©2009VM Wolter · Blue Creek School Building, El Campo, TX
Joseph attended first through fourth grades in this little country school off FM
1162 before the family moved to the Newton Addition, a community called Red
Hill, just south of El Campo.

©2009VM Wolter   Hiding Bridge, El Campo, TX
On the days Joseph missed the school bus, he walked this long gravel road to
the Blue Creek School. There were times he hid underneath this bridge and did
not go to school.

©2009VM Wolter   Workhouses, FM 1300 TX

The Workhouses

Living in the country was a life much different than living in, or near, a town. Much of our food came from our own resources. From the cattle came meat (beef), milk, and butter; from the chickens, we had eggs and poultry; we raised hogs for our bacon, hams, pan and link sausage, hog-head cheese, and more. This was just the way of living in the country during my early childhood days in the 1940s and 1950s.

The workhouses seen in this photograph hold many memories from those yesteryear days. The house on the left was always called the deep-freeze house. Many of the memories of this house are filled with processing chickens.

Mama raised a lot of chickens. I remember one day we processed over one hundred chickens. My job, along with my younger sister and the two sons of another family, was to pluck the feathers and pinfeathers from the scalded, and very smelly, chicken and pass it to my Uncle Johnny, Aunt Hazel, Dad, or Mama for them to complete the task necessary for processing the chickens, and to clean all the gizzards. (One note here about the stench that comes from a scalded chicken. Once you've smelled it, you will never forget it! It's worse than smelling a dirty, wet dog!) "How's your appetite now? Anyone for some fried chicken?"

Once all this was done, the meat was wrapped in special wrapping paper, called freezer paper or waxed paper, and the processed chickens were placed in the big deep freeze that sat at one end of the house—giving the name of deep-freeze house to this building. Now let's look at the other house—the smokehouse.

At the sign of the first cold weather, Daddy would get up before the crack of dawn, put on his denim overalls, chambray shirt, boots, and heavy coat and would build a large fire outdoors. He'd set a huge barrel over the fire and fill it with water.

He would then rope a chosen hog, kill it, and, using a pulley-wrench, lift the heavy porker into the heated water, which made it easier to scrape the hair clean from the hog. I can still recall the disgusting odor. It's a wonder we could even eat any meat!

After the scraping came the butchering, hams to be cured, sausage to be made and smoked, and pickling of pig feet. Mama used the head and other parts to make hog-head cheese—I STILL don't see why it's called cheese!

The small house sat upon cement blocks, and having no windows and only one door, it was used to smoke and cure the meat. Daddy would get a bucket to build a fire. He used green wood to make smoke. If there wasn't any around, he would use the tree limbs and, on the hot coals, lay wet moss from the oak trees surrounding our home. He would then tend to the meat for about two weeks.

(VMW)

The Writer

It's a cold, cloudy late Sunday evening. The radiance from the lights on my Christmas tree gives a soft glow to the room. Never mind the fact that it's mid-June; I leave my tree up year round.

The scene is set; all preparations have been made to have everything perfect for words to be written on pages of time—words that flow from this writer's heart and will captivate readers, young and old.

The all-necessary coffee to keep the eyes open, the perfect instrumental CD and headset to inspire and stimulate the mind. Ahh, yes, let the writing begin!

What's this? The writer thinks. Why is it that interruptions have to occur? Why, with seven days in a week, twenty-four hours in the day, does someone choose this moment to vacuum?

Is this a test or trial writers have to face? Where can one go to escape? I must focus! Shutting out the noise, turning the music a bit louder, I try to focus on the music and listen carefully.

Oh, yes, I can now see more clearly, scenes in my imagination. Scenes flow back and forth, causing me, the writer, to feel the need to write, to put on paper what flows from my most inner self.

I see warriors of old on their gallant steeds as they face each other. They are fully clad in their armor, spear in hand, and each clutching his bridle reins. The signal is given!

Each warrior charges toward his opponent in the hope of being the winner. The winner's prize is the hand of the fair maiden they both love. Yet, only one can be left straddling his gallant steed.

Facing each other, they charge forth. Crash! One is knocked to one side of his saddle, but not off his mount; he's still in the game!

Again they face each other—again the horses charge forward. The tension of the crowd grows as they reach the point of impact.

Alas, one warrior's lance finds its mark, sending his opponent sprawling to the ground. He has defeated his opponent and won the hand of the fair maiden.

Who is this mysterious warrior who could defeat his worthy opponent? He dismounts, walks toward the king to claim his prize—none other than the love of his life, Lady Gwinn.

Bowing before the king, he removes his helmet. Everyone is astonished to see the winner's face—everyone except Lady Gwinn. She steps forward...

The whirling sound from the vacuum can still be heard as the CD ends and so does this prose. Such goes only a small portion of the day in the life of this busy writer. (VMW)

Highway Cowboy

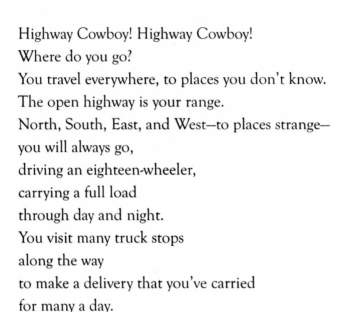

Highway Cowboy! Highway Cowboy!
Where do you go?
You travel everywhere, to places you don't know.
The open highway is your range.
North, South, East, and West—to places strange—
you will always go,
driving an eighteen-wheeler,
carrying a full load
through day and night.
You visit many truck stops
along the way
to make a delivery that you've carried
for many a day.

Highway Cowboy! Highway Cowboy!
Where do you drive today?
When you arrive, where will you stay?
Will you stay in a motel?
Or, will you sleep inside your cab
until the break of dawn?
Highway Cowboy! Highway Cowboy!
You're always on the go.
Here today, gone tomorrow.
There's many a mile you will travel
far away from home,
doing what you do best, being free to roam.

From southern Texas, you've come
to the far reaches of eastern states.
You've passed many a truck.
Highway Cowboy, many are your risks
for unsatisfactory pay.
Bumper jumpers, tailgaters, and people
cutting you off are all serious peril to you.
Through the narrow blacktop roads,
through rain, snow, sleet, and sunshine,
you're always on the go.
Highway Cowboy! Highway Cowboy!
Your destiny travels with you
through many a sleepless night
as you strive to make a living
the best way you possibly can.

Highway Cowboy! Highway Cowboy!
You're older now, tired and weary.
Maybe it's time you hang it up
and come back home where you belong
because that open highway gets longer every year.
Why not make that next run your last one?
Come back home! Cowboy, come on back home!
Put your trailer aside, you've done your job.
Give your life a chance, live it for a change.
Highway Cowboy! Highway Cowboy!
Come on home. Come on home. (JAZ)

The Eagle

How high the noble eagle flies
against the splendor
of the majestic blue skies.
Against the background of white clouds,
he soars gracefully.
The lone eagle in the sky
reigns supreme in his solitude
and freedom, this bird of prey,
his ever watchful eye scanning
as he searches the ground below
for prey and danger of man.

The eagle in flight
is perpetual beauty in motion,
kept in sight as far as the eye can see.
The magnificent bird,
with widespread wings, sharp claws
and a shrill screech, can be heard
from the distance.
He captures his prey
and flies toward his silent refuge,
which nature provides,
free from intrusion.

This is our American eagle,
America's symbol of our freedom.
As long as this beautiful bird soars

high above in the heavenly sky,
soaring watchful and vigilant
in his flight,
his stature as a bird of prey
will never diminish
with each passing day. (JAZ)

A New Year's Reflection

There is a quarter moon out tonight,
on this cold January evening.
Only a few stars are within sight.
It is New Year's Day.
A forceful wind blows
and windows in the house creak softly.
No one knows how long winter will last—
perhaps until spring or beyond.

The New Year's arrival
brings resolutions to be made.
The passage of time cannot be stopped.
How we live it is another matter.
Procrastination doesn't help!
There's uneasiness we feel
as the early January days
pass. We look toward the future
with optimism and renewal. (JAZ)

His Way Isn't Our Way

In I Corinthians 15, Paul writes about Christ's resurrection and faith's reality and how—if Christ wasn't raised we wouldn't be either. If that were true then his preaching was in vain, as is our faith. But, Praise God, Christ did rise from the grave, thereby giving us hope and a promise of our being resurrected, as well. I say, "Glory to God!"

I read in II Corinthians where Paul writes these letters as a way to let us know that it can be exciting to serve the Lord, but, that being a Christian *can* lead to pain and suffering.

After reading this, I thought of a good friend. She was a godly woman who, after turning ninety years old, learned that she had cancer.

She suffered a lot in such a short time after learning about her cancer and, at the end, questioned God as to why she had to suffer so much pain. She asked me, "Why doesn't the Lord just take me?" To this, I had no answer.

One would think if one had lived a good Christian life, serving the Lord, that He would make death easier by just taking one to heaven and bypassing pain and suffering.

Nevertheless, I say that God's ways are not our ways. Everything is in His own time and for His purpose. It's all a great mystery to me. (VMW)

The Caregiver

Lord, it's been too long since our last visit, at no fault of Yours—it's me. I ask for forgiveness for being preoccupied and for allowing "stuff" to come between us, stealing my time from You.

It's not easy being a caregiver and providing help to another person. The emotional and physical strain I feel sometimes causes me to become frustrated and angry.

There is the feeling of guilt, thinking I should be able to provide better care even though I know I'm doing my very best.

My social life is shot, and I am so lonely; I feel I'm on an island, and it is about to sink out of sight and no one will ever know. Perhaps they won't even miss me! I wonder.

I'm exhausted when I go to bed at night and when I get up. The days are long, seemingly endless. I have no energy to do what I must, but I do it anyway because I have to; there is no choice in the matter. I feel tired all the time!

I feel overwhelmed with the duties of being a caregiver, and I no longer have interest in activities I used to enjoy. There was a time I had friends, did crafts, even founded WIN (Women In Need), a ministry for women, and published a monthly newsletter, but all of this is gone.

Depression and anger have fallen upon me, and I feel sad a lot, but I know I must continue caring for my loved one. People ask, "How's your mother?" But does anyone ever ask about the caregiver? They do not! (VMW)

The Ninth Inning

It was bottom of the ninth inning.
The score was tied at six to six.
The Yankees and the Indians were playing
in front of a large crowd in Yankee Stadium.
What a slugfest it was!
There were two outs, a Yankee on second base,
and number seven in the Yankee's batting order
stood menacingly at the plate.
With a three ball, two strikes on him,
a tense, anxious crowd watched and waited.

Moose stood,
glaring defiantly at the Indians' pitcher,
determined to end this ballgame once and for all.
Both sides of benched players and managers
watched anxiously—
as the runner prepared for the unexpected.
Even the crowd sat in eerie silence.
It had come down to one pitch.
All through eight and one-half innings of hard-
fought baseball from the first through the ninth
inning, it was touch and go for both sides,
one ball game the fans would never forget.
Now, it was a battle of strong wills
between pitcher and batter
to see who would really win.

The pitcher was ready with nerves of steel,
a wicked glint in his eye; he began to wind up.
The Moose stood calm and collected,
watching the pitcher.
The silence in the stadium was unbearable
as Skowron clenched his bat tightly.
His jaw tightened as he watched
the ball come toward him.
It was a 95 mph fastball—Moose was ready.
He swung his mighty bat viciously.
Crack! Ball against bat
and the ball soared out of sight.
Moose knew it was a home run
as he cleared the bases.

The score was eight to six!
The roar of the tumultuous crowd was deafening
as they stood up to watch their beloved Yankees,
Skowron, Mantle, and all the rest,
take their bows because they were the best.
The Cleveland Indians lost a great game that day,
but they would come back another day.
For now, the baseball gods smiled on the Moose,
Mantle, and Maris.
The Yankees were on their way,
but it would be a long time
before Yankee and Indians fans would forget
this ninth inning at Yankee Stadium. (JAZ)

The Writer's Ode

Writers experience stress,
just like basketball players
in a full court press.
For the writer with creative imagination
must also strive to avoid writer's block.
He must write, write, and write
into the dead of night and into early morn.
He or she must keep their dream alive
and no clock or calendar will prevent
the writer from seeking his goal.

Success is there if you try.
Failure lurks with every rejection slip,
but you never hesitate once you start,
because your writing is in your heart.
From start to finish no matter what you write,
every successful step you take
will put you in the limelight.
For every step of the way,
you and your imagination strive
for the very best you can be.
Then, in due time, then and only then,
you'll have realized your ultimate goal.
Not every writer is successful.
Without effort, your reward is minimal,
but the satisfaction is great.
Through your individual achievement,

the ultimate reward is being published.
Time and patience, skill and development
all are part of the game.
You see, the literary world is a tough one.
Only you, the writer, know what to do. (JAZ)

Life's Reality

Life's tragic moments come when someone wants to deprive you of them. For life's reality consists of strife in our world, which seems to thrive on humanity against humanity, sanity against insanity.

You ask this question over and over: "Has the world gone mad!" Everyone reads the papers with headlines emblazoning violence at its worst, reporting very little on the good that does occur, and yet, the world marches forward.

The tragedy of life's reality! Every day is filled with an experience you remember or prefer to forget. Life, in today's world, is a struggle for survival. The strong will survive, the weak will fall behind, and through it all, in living life, no one escapes the harshness of life's reality. (JAZ)

Wolves That Run in the Forest

Alone and free, in the wilderness
roams a wolf and his mate.
By night and day, they roam;
the wilderness is their home.
Far from prying eyes, they hunt for prey.
Sometimes they prowl, hungry along the way.
But nature provides food and wild game
for them to survive.

They are wary of human eyes as
they search for water along creek beds or streams.
In the dead of night, underneath a full moon,
you can hear their mournful howl.
Wolves run in the forest thick,
always cautious and on the prowl.
The woods are their protection,
their only domain.
Spring, summer, fall, and winter
the wolf and his mate continue to roam.

Amidst the solitude and peace,
I, a lone Indian, live in a white man's cabin,
by choice.
Only the great Manitou in the sky and
the wolves that prowl hear my lonely voice.
Freedom is mine to enjoy.
I, the proud Indian, once was a young boy.

My friends, the deer and the bear, much like the
wolves, listen to the winds that change
and to many sounds that are strange.

Many a winter will come and go
and with spring, the melting of the snow.
Summer will come and the
leaves will turn green.
The wolf and his mate once again roam;
for them, winter was rather lean.
This lonely warrior is content with his lot.
When the great Manitou calls,
only nature's leaves will cover my body,
while lying in my favorite spot—
the wolves will continue to run in the forest. (JAZ)

The Helmet

Sometimes it is not easy to live the Christian life. Satan is always at
one's heels. He slips his thoughts into one's mind and the battle
begins!

This is where the helmet of salvation is so important! If a believer
wears the helmet of salvation, or is secure in his salvation, then
Satan cannot enter his mind. (VMW)

*"Therefore, put on every piece of God's armor so you will be able to resist
the enemy in the time of evil. Then after the battle you will still be standing
firm." Ephesians 6:13*

A Man of Honor

Old and stooped, this eighty-year-old
Gentleman lives alone, surrounded by memories.
His family has left home. His beloved wife
Now rests in the arms of the Lord—
But he is a proud man, sitting in silence.
He is a man of honor.

The twinkle in his eyes remains, when he smiles.
He will shake your hand firmly,
Greeting you with a pleasant hug.
His hearing is on the verge of deafness
As he strains to hear every word.
This is a man of honor.

Once upon a time, he was a Knight of Columbus,
In his younger days. He helped one and all,
Giving unselfishly of himself
In service to God and country.
He was undaunted, this man of honor!

He opened his heart to many,
Consoled the young and the old,
This gallant Knight, a true soldier of Christ!
Sacrifice on his part made many happy.
This was his calling because God was on his side.
Yes, he was a noble and humble man.

I went to see him one wintery day.
I sat beside him; we recalled our past,
Praying for all our loved ones,
their families, and our church and community.

He spoke slowly, his voice echoing
In a room once filled with love, laughter,
And family.
I hung onto every word,
Thinking of how I was once lost,
And found my way back—
To find myself a soldier of Christ.
Thanks to this man of honor.

Many years have passed.
Time has changed since that last visit;
A visit I'll always cherish.
Deep in my heart, I'll remember this kind
And gentle man who has joined the ranks
As a soldier of Christ, in heaven.
Someday we'll meet again, the old man and I,
And together we shall be remembered
As men of honor. (JAZ)

What Is a Father?

He's strength and security
Laughter and fun
A prince to his daughter
A pal to his son
A great storyteller
And mender of toys
Who's seldom dismayed
By the family's noise.
He's a man to consult
When a problem arises
As eager a worker as there'll ever be
Who wants all the best
For his whole family.
He's a loving instructor
Who struggles to teach
His child to achieve
All the goals one could reach
And he knows in his heart
That it's worth all the bother
When he hears his child say
"That man? He's <u>my</u> father!"

—Donna M. Neal

God Was For Her—
Who Could Be Against Her?
A Tribute to Edna

She was given no awards for having been one of the world's greatest moms, but she should have, and if she hasn't she will one day receive a greater award through God.

Edna was the third of eight children born to Coyet and Lillie Lee McKey. She grew up along the banks of the Navidad River near Vienna, Texas and twenty miles from Hallettsville where not one of the children ever forgot old Brother King and his preaching of fire and damnation or the baptizing in the river.

We all eventually (except Elvie) moved away from Vienna. It seems to me, old Brother King never once let go of any of us eight children. Through Edna's adult life, she drew many times from his teachings.

"Come unto me all ye who are weary and heavy laden and I will give you rest."

As a very young girl, Edna left grade school and our family. She took a job for a Doctor Satterfield (near Cuero or Runge). Living in their home, she helped care for his invalid wife. She sent money home to help the family. Edna was very good at working with the sick and in the years to come Daddy sent for Edna many times. "Come home. Mom is ill and we need help."

Edna was a beautiful young woman. Tall with blond hair and big blue eyes. She had taken from Daddy, his bright blue eyes and from Mom her beautiful skin.

The family had known Henry for years and while away from home working for the doctor, Edna and Henry's paths were to cross again.

Henry, dark, good-looking, and much older than Edna, had a charming personality and was liked by almost everyone—that is except our mom. He was an excellent rancher, painter, and cook. Henry could get a job where no one else could! I remember he rode a fine white horse and was often seen with a roll of money as big as his fist.

Edna fell deeply in love with Henry and married him against Mom's will! She would have laid down her life for him, and did so eight times while Henry delivered, with no medical training and no pain-relieving drugs, their eight children. With each of them, Edna had no prenatal care. Much of the time there was not enough food, let alone a good healthy diet. Today, though Edna is deceased, she gave to this world eight beautiful, healthy, happy children. God was for her; who could be against her?

During the birth of the last child, Edna all but gave her life. Henry had always drank and by this time he was deeply into alcohol. Edna had long ago become a victim of domestic abuse at his hands. Edna, in a weakened condition, could not give birth this time without the help of a good doctor. Her labor went on and on. She began to bleed excessively—then hemorrhaged profusely! Something or someone moved Henry to get an ambulance, reaching the hospital with barely enough time to save Edna and the beautiful little girl.

They had seven girls and one boy. Early in their marriage Henry was a good husband and father. As the babies kept coming, Edna's health began to fail. She couldn't take it anymore, even though she knew one word and Henry would slap or kick her around or break a chair over her. As this last child was five or six years old, Henry became so abusive to Edna, she felt she had to leave once and for all. The older children wouldn't stand for any more abuse of their mother. During the last summer I spent with her, I ran a few blocks to call the law more than once or twice, as Edna huddled in a corner, protecting her head and face as he broke up more than one chair over her back. Too little too late but Edna may have left him long ago except Mom hadn't exactly said to her, "Our door will always be open to you."

Edna made the break only when she saw and believed their older children would do something really bad to Henry. They would not watch him abuse her anymore. I never once saw Henry abuse the children.

Edna made a home for eight children, a young girl she took in years earlier, and herself on a waitress' salary!

I am so thankful, while during our last summer together, I taught Edna how to count money and make change. The cash registers didn't do it for you in those days. Getting out on her own was very hard for her, but with this little bit of knowledge she was able to get a job. She enjoyed some of her life and near the end she managed quite a large restaurant in Houston.

Forgiving Henry—I never once believed I could forgive or forget his abuse to Edna. I was to see him again, though, years later. He was old by then and had suffered major strokes and was almost an invalid. But, he still knew me, and I knew then I had never really hated him. He wept as he tried to speak. In his eyes, I knew he wanted to say if he could only have one more chance. At this time I felt compassion for him. I had never believed I could. Edna forgave him. She even helped him along the way once many years after the divorce. That's how Edna was. She judged no one!

And though Henry is gone on now to meet his maker, did God forgive him? Yes, I know he did! Because that's how God is. Today, Edna and Henry rest side by side in Willow Creek Cemetery near Vienna and near Mom and Dad. And side by side, I think rightfully so. Edna had a deep love for Henry to the end. And I believe Henry loved her. But that's alcohol for you and what it will do. And that's right back to our teachings by Old Brother King and our mom. Edna faced death with the same quiet determination she faced life.

(Written with great admiration for Edna by her youngest sister, Elsie, on April 4, 1996.)

—Elsie McKey Overstreet

Love Letters to Jesus Journal

The following blank pages will provide you with an opportunity to journal your thoughts and feelings as you see God's plan unfold in your life. You might think of this section as your journal in which to write "Love Letters to Jesus" that reflect your deepest thoughts.

Contributors

Donna M. Neal, the youngest of four children, was born in Texas, raised in Kansas and Oregon, and was the daughter of a minister. She is retired from her position as verification clerk in a claims department for medical billing and now is juggling her time between watching sports and doing various crafts. She also enjoys drawing, corresponding with pen pals, and writing, and has a great love for animals.

Elsie McKey Overstreet was raised in Lavaca County near the Navidad River, the youngest of eight children. She graduated head of her class in Vocational Nursing from Del Mar College in Corpus Christi, Texas—now retired. She is a mother to one daughter, grandmother to one granddaughter, and great-grandmother to two girls and four boys. Her writing comes from a "burning in her heart," and she has a great love for animals.

For the Homeless
and the Hurting

While writing this book, we were moved to do something to help those less fortunate—the homeless and the hurting.

Our publishers at Outskirts Press are joining us in donating 25 cents from each book sold, to organizations that support the hurting and the homeless. By purchasing this book you have contributed 25 cents to worthy causes across the United States.

Thank you for participating in this work.

"For I was hungry, and you fed me. I was thirsty, and you gave me a drink. I was a stranger, and you invited me into your home. I was naked, and you gave me clothing. I was sick, and you cared for me. I was in prison, and you visited me.—I tell you the truth, when you did it to one of the least of these, my brothers and sister, you were doing it to me!" Matthew 25:35-36, 40

Notes

If you would like to contribute stories for our
upcoming book entitled

Rockin Chair Cowboys:
And Other Short Stories

Please send them to the following address:
V. M. Wolter
P. O. Box 722405
Houston, Texas 77272

These stories must be your original story and not taken from
other material. They must be stories that touch the heart and
soul with the flavor of "remember when."
For each story, please give your name, address, and phone num-
ber. We will not be able to contact everyone who submits a
story, but will certainly notify you if the story you submit is used.
Manuscripts and photocopies cannot be returned.

*"Father, I pray that You will bless our readers and keep them; that You
will make Your face to shine upon them, and be gracious to them; that
You will lift up Your countenance upon them, and give them peace."*
Amen

LaVergne, TN USA
17 September 2009
158229LV00003B/6/P